~MEETING FAMOUS PEOPLE~

Muhammad Ali
Meet the Champion

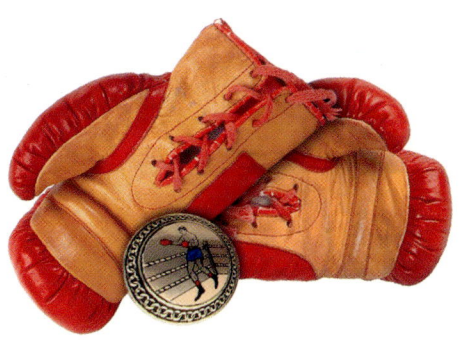

Denise M. Jordan

Enslow Publishers, Inc.
40 Industrial Road   PO Box 38
Box 398   Aldershot
Berkeley Heights, NJ 07922   Hants GU12 6BP
USA   UK
http://www.enslow.com

Copyright © 2003 by Enslow Publishers, Inc.

All rights reserved.

No part of this book may be reproduced by any means without the written permission of the publisher.

Library of Congress Cataloging-in-Publication Data

Jordan, Denise.
   Muhammad Ali : meet the champion / Denise M. Jordan.
      v. cm. — (Meeting famous people)
   Contents: An early start—Training to win—"The Greatest"—The champ fights back—The biggest challenge.
   ISBN 0-7660-2272-2 (hardcover)
   1. Ali, Muhammad, 1942– .—Juvenile literature. 2. Boxers (Sports)—United States—Biography—Juvenile literature. [1. Ali, Muhammad, 1942– . 2. Boxers (Sports) 3. African Americans—Biography.] I. Title. II. Series.
   GV1132.A4J67 2003
   796.83'092—dc21

                                                                           2002154650

Printed in the United States of America

10 9 8 7 6 5 4 3 2 1

To Our Readers: We have done our best to make sure all Internet Addresses in this book were active and appropriate when we went to press. However, the author and the publisher have no control over and assume no liability for the material available on those Internet sites or on other Web sites they may link to. Any comments or suggestions can be sent by e-mail to comments@enslow.com or to the address on the back cover.

Every effort has been made to locate all copyright holders of material used in this book. If any errors or omissions have occurred, corrections will be made in future editions of this book.

Illustration Credits: AP/MSG, p. 4; AP/Wide World Photos, pp. 7, 8, 11, 14, 17, 18, 19, 20, 22, 23, 24, 26, 27, 28, 30; © The Courier-Journal, p. 12; Library of Congress, p. 3; Photo by Robert L. Haggins, p. 16.

Cover Illustration: AP/Wide World Photos

```
J 92 A399jo 2003
Jordan, Denise.
Muhammad Ali : meet the
champion
```

Table of Contents

1. An Early Start 5

2. Training to Win 10

3. "The Greatest" 15

4. The Champ Fights Back 21

5. The Biggest Challenge 25

Timeline 29

Words to Know 30

Learn More About Muhammad Ali 31
   (Books and Internet Addresses)

Index 32

Cassius Clay later changed his name to Muhammad Ali.

Chapter 1

An Early Start

Cassius Clay, Jr., looked up and down the street. Where was his bicycle? He had parked it outside the building—and now it was gone. Cassius asked a policeman for help. Then Cassius said that he wanted to beat up the person who stole his new bike.

The policeman was Officer Joe Martin. He also taught boxing at a nearby gym. He said, "You thinking about beating somebody up, you had better learn to fight." A few days later, twelve-year-old Cassius went to the Columbia Gym for his first boxing lesson.

That was just the start for the boy who grew up to become one of the most exciting fighters in the world of boxing.

Cassius Clay, Jr., was born January 17, 1942, in Louisville, Kentucky. His parents were Odessa and Cassius Clay, Sr. When little Cassius was two years old, his brother, Rudolph, was born.

> **Cassius was so mad when his brand-new bike was stolen.**

In those days, African Americans were not treated fairly. They were kept apart from white people. They could not eat in the same restaurants or shop in the same stores. Their children went to separate schools and played in separate parks. Blacks and whites could not

Louisville, where Cassius grew up, is the biggest city in Kentucky.

sit together on buses or in movie theaters. All this made Cassius very sad.

Cassius's father worked painting signs and billboards. He also painted large pictures on the walls of many Baptist churches. Cassius's mother cleaned and cooked in the homes of rich white people.

As a boy, Cassius liked to shoot marbles in the dirt with his friends. He also liked to watch the race horses. Louisville is well known for the Kentucky Derby, a horse race held every year. Sometimes, when the trainers ran the horses around the track, Cassius tried to

> Cassius, left, was the "hardest worker of any kid I ever taught," said Officer Joe Martin.

run faster than the horses. On Sunday mornings, Cassius went to church with his family. He often sang in the children's choir.

After his bicycle was stolen, Cassius started taking boxing lessons from Officer Joe Martin. Cassius learned to move around the ring. He learned how to throw punches and keep from getting hit. He jumped rope and lifted weights to build his muscles. He decided he would never smoke or drink alcohol. He would eat only good foods to keep his body healthy.

Some days, Cassius got up at 4 o'clock in the morning and went running for two hours before school. Other days, he raced against the school bus. The kids on the bus laughed when they saw Cassius running next to the bus. Cassius did not care. He was training to be a champion.

Chapter 2

Training to Win

When Cassius was sixteen, he felt bold enough to fight the neighborhood bully. This boy had beat up Cassius and many of his friends. One day, he challenged the bully to a fight in the Columbia Gym. Cassius punched him in the nose and sent him running home. Cassius's friends cheered and lifted him up on their shoulders. He was the new "king" of the neighborhood.

Cassius did not work as hard in school as he did in the gym. Sometimes he did his homework, and sometimes he did not. He played around in the halls and told jokes in class. He almost missed graduating with the rest of his class at Central High School in 1960.

By the time Cassius was eighteen, he had won many important boxing matches. He had won the Kentucky Golden Glove tournament six times. He had won the national Golden Glove championship twice. He held two national Amateur

Cassius has always been close friends with his brother, Rudy, left.

Athletic Union (AAU) titles. Cassius had won 100 out of 108 fights. He was ready for bigger challenges.

Cassius earned a spot on the United States Olympic Team in 1960. In the Olympic boxing matches, Cassius won a gold medal.

Cassius bragged all the time. He made up poems and told jokes about other boxers. He said he could beat heavyweight champion Sonny Liston. Cassius trained hard to make this dream come true.

He worked on his hand and foot speed. He punched or jabbed the other boxer, then stepped away. He danced around the ring,

Cassius was proud to wear his Olympic jacket.

moving back and forth and side to side. His favorite saying was, "Float like a butterfly, sting like a bee!" Cassius moved in, landed a stinging blow, then floated away. "I am the Greatest!" he said.

Some people thought Cassius's bragging was funny. Others did not like his jokes or his poetry. Many newspaper writers said Cassius talked too much. They wanted someone to knock him out.

Cassius got his chance to fight the heavyweight champion in 1964. Sonny Liston was a strong fighter, but he could not stop Cassius Clay. Cassius danced around the ring. He jabbed with his left, threw a punch with his right, then floated away.

Sonny Liston gave up in the seventh round. Cassius jumped about the ring, shouting, "I am the Greatest!" Cassius Clay, age twenty-two, was the new heavyweight champion of the world.

"I can't be beat!" Cassius roared with excitement when he won the heavyweight title.

Chapter 3

"The Greatest"

In his private time, Cassius listened to the speeches of Malcolm X. He was a preacher in the Nation of Islam. Members of the Nation of Islam said that white people treated black people badly. They said blacks should stay away from whites. They told African Americans to be proud of being black.

Some people called the Nation of Islam a hate group. They did not want Cassius to be in this

Cassius, center, learned about the Nation of Islam from Malcolm X, left.

religious group. Still, Cassius joined the Nation of Islam. Then he changed his name to Muhammad Ali. *Muhammad* means "one worthy of praise." *Ali* was the name of a great general.

Often, people in the Nation of Islam chose new names. Their old names made them remember that long ago, black people had been forced to be slaves—and slaves were given names by their owners. Taking a new name felt like a new beginning.

Ali began to speak out about his beliefs. He said that African Americans should fight back when they were treated unfairly. He said that the United States should not send soldiers to fight a war in the country of Vietnam. He said that all people around the world should learn to live in peace.

Ali also continued to box and defend his heavyweight title. He fought a rematch with Sonny Liston in 1965. Several months later, he fought against Floyd Patterson. Ali won this match, too. He was still the heavyweight champion of the world.

Then Ali got into trouble with the government. In 1967, all men age eighteen or older had to sign up for military service. Many of them were sent to fight in Vietnam.

Ali gave speeches to talk about ideas that were important to him.

Ali refused to join the army. It was against his religion to fight in a war, he said.

The government did not believe Ali. He was called a traitor and a coward. In court, he was found guilty of refusing to serve in the army.

> Again, in 1965, Ali beat Liston.

His punishment was a $10,000 fine and five years in prison. His heavyweight title and his boxing license were taken away. For Ali, this was a terrible blow.

Ali asked the Supreme Court—which is the highest court in the country—to rule on his case. He did not have to stay in jail during this time, but he could not fight any boxing matches. Three long years later, the

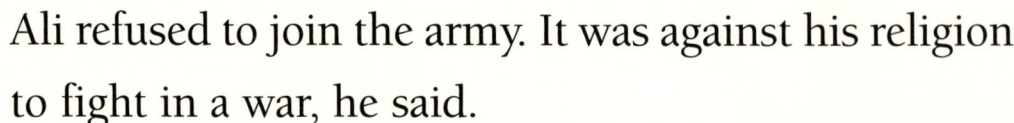

Supreme Court ruled that Ali had been treated unfairly. Because of his deep religious beliefs, he did not have to join the army. He did not have to pay the fine or go to jail. And he could have his boxing license back. At last, Ali could box again.

Even so, all of Ali's problems were not over. A new heavyweight champ had been crowned during the years when Ali could not box. Joe Frazier was the new champion. Ali would have to fight Frazier for the title. But first, Ali would have to win some other fights.

Many fans agreed that Ali should not join the army.

Ali did not fight for almost four years. Now he had to train hard to get his speed and his strength back.

Chapter 4

The Champ Fights Back

Could Ali win again? At age twenty-nine, were his best boxing years over? Ali's first match was with Jerry Quarry in 1970. Ali beat Quarry easily. He won against other boxers, too. Still, his time off from boxing showed. He threw hard punches, but he was not as quick as he used to be.

On March 8, 1971, Ali got his chance to fight Joe Frazier. It was a long, hard fight, and Ali lost. This

March 8, 1971: Ali was down. Frazier had won the match.

was the first time Ali lost a fight since he had turned pro. Three years passed before Ali got the chance to fight Frazier again. On January 28, 1974, Ali whipped Frazier in the twelfth round.

Still, this win did not mean that Ali was the world champion. Another boxer, George Foreman, was now the champ. Ali would have to fight Foreman to get the title back.

On October 30, 1974, Ali got his chance to fight Foreman. The fight took place in Zaire, Africa. It was called the "Rumble in the Jungle."

Ali knocked out George Foreman in the eighth round. The crowd went wild. People screamed and chanted, "Ali! Ali! Ali!" Ali had proved again that he was "the Greatest." He had regained the heavyweight championship title.

Joe Frazier tried to win the title back in 1975 at a fight in the Philippine Islands. This famous fight between the two champions was called "The Thrilla in Manila." Ali and Frazier pounded each other. Finally, Frazier gave up. Ali was still the "Champ."

Ali remained champion until 1978,

Ali holds his trophy after the "Thrilla in Manila." With him are his father, right, and his brother.

when he lost his title to Leon Spinks. Spinks had won an Olympic gold medal in 1976. He was in great shape and many years younger than Ali.

Ali tried to knock Spinks out, but he could not. He tried to tire Spinks out, but Spinks would not quit. When the fight was over, Spinks was the winner.

Ali was ashamed of his loss to Spinks. Ali believed he lost the fight because he had not trained well. He asked for a rematch. The next time, he would be ready.

Ali defeated Spinks easily on September 15, 1978. Once again, he proved that he was "the Greatest." Ali was the first boxer to win the world heavyweight title three times.

Ali always liked to test his speed. Here he ran next to some horses.

Chapter 5

The Biggest Challenge

Ali decided it was time to quit boxing. Men usually box their best between the ages of twenty and thirty. Ali was thirty-eight. He wanted to stop boxing while he was still the "Champ."

But Ali could not sit still. It was too quiet. He was used to training, traveling, and boxing. He wanted to fight again. In 1980, he lost a match against boxer Larry Holmes. He lost another fight a short time later to Trevor Berbick. Ali was too old to box and win.

"I'm finished," Ali said. "Father Time caught up with me." This time, Ali stopped boxing for good.

When Ali was about forty years old, he noticed that something was wrong when he talked. His words often ran together. People had trouble understanding what he said. His hands trembled, and his movements were slow and stiff.

In 1984, after seeing many doctors and taking lots of medical tests, Ali was told that he had Parkinson's disease. It was causing all his problems.

No one knows how Ali got Parkinson's. Some experts believe that punches to the

After he stopped boxing, Ali learned that he had Parkinson's.

head from boxing may have caused it. Other older boxers have similar problems with speaking and moving. Ali visits his doctors and takes medicine to help control the disease.

Ali has been married four times and has seven daughters and two sons. He and his wife, Yolanda, live on a ranch in Michigan.

Ali with his wife, Yolanda, who is called Lonnie.

The 1996 Summer Olympic Games took place in Atlanta, Georgia. The Olympics bring together people of all nations. Muhammad Ali was the perfect choice for lighting the torch to start the festivities. He was known all over the world as an athlete—and also as a strong believer in world peace and understanding. He always had the courage to say and do what he thought was right. The crowd cheered when Ali appeared on the stage. Chants of "Ali! Ali! Ali!" filled the stadium.

In 2002, Ali held the Olympic torch in Salt Lake City.

Parkinson's has slowed him down, but Ali has not lost his sense of humor, his love of life, and his deep faith in the Nation of Islam. Ali still works to help others. He travels to raise money to cure diseases and to bring food and medicine to poor children around the world. Ali is the best-known sports hero of all time. He has been photographed, talked about, written about, and argued about more than any other athlete in the world. Awards and honors fill his home. Muhammad Ali is still the "People's Champion."

Timeline

1942~Born in Louisville, Kentucky, on January 17.

1960~Wins a gold medal at the Olympics in Rome, Italy.

1964~Beats Sonny Liston to become heavyweight champion of the world. Joins the Nation of Islam and changes his name to Muhammad Ali.

1967~Refuses to join the army because of his religious beliefs. His boxing license is taken away.

1970~United States Supreme Court rules Ali was treated unfairly. He can fight again.

1974~Knocks out George Foreman to become heavyweight champ for the second time.

1978~Loses heavyweight title to Leon Spinks, then wins it back in a rematch.

1981~Retires from boxing. Spends more time working for world peace and raising money for charity.

1984~Learns that he has Parkinson's disease.

2003~Continues to travel around the country to raise money to help other people.

Words to Know

Amateur Athletic Union—An organization of athletes playing sports for fun.

Golden Glove—An organization for young boxers in the United States.

heavyweight—A boxer who weighs more than 190 pounds.

Nation of Islam—A group of black people, also called Black Muslims, who follow parts of the Islam religion and believe that blacks should stay separate from whites.

Olympic Games—Contests for athletes from all over the world to compete for medals.

Parkinson's disease—A brain disorder that makes a person lose muscle control.

slave—A person who is treated like property and can be bought or sold.

Vietnam—A country in Southeast Asia.

Learn More

Books

Garret, Leslie. *The Story of Muhammad Ali*.
   New York: Dorling Kindersley, 2002.

Haskins, James. *The Story of Muhammad Ali*.
   New York: Walker and Company, 2002.

Hook, Jason. *Muhammad Ali: The Greatest*.
   Austin, Tex.: Raintree Steck-Vaughn, 2001.

Shange, Ntozake. *Float Like a Butterfly*.
   New York: Hyperion Books for Children, 2002.

Internet Addresses

Ali's hometown newspaper has articles, photos, and links.
   <http://www.courier-journal.com/ali>

Read more about Ali at this sports Web site.
   <http://www.hickoksports.com/biograph/
   alimuham.shtml>

You'll find lots of great photos here.
   <http://www.mxdpi.com/main/index.cgi?direct=
   ATHLETES/Muhammad_Ali>

Index

A
Ali, Muhammad
  birth, 6
  childhood, 5–11
  education, 11
  heavyweight champion, 13, 14, 17, 23–24
  learns to fight, 6, 9
  marriages, 27
  name change, 16
  Olympics, 12, 27–28
  Parkinson's, 26–27, 28
  training, 9, 12–13, 20
  war protest, 17–18
Amateur Athletic Union (AAU), 11–12

B
Berbick, Trevor, 26

C
Clay, Cassius Jr. (*See* Ali, Muhammad)
Clay, Cassius Sr. (father), 6, 8
Clay, Odessa (mother), 6, 8
Clay, Rudolph (brother), 6, 11

F
Foreman, George, 22–23
Frazier, Joe, 19, 21–22, 23

G
Golden Glove championship, 11

H
Holmes, Larry, 25

K
Kentucky Derby, 8
Kentucky Golden Glove, 11

L
Liston, Sonny, 12, 13, 17
Louisville, Kentucky, 6, 7, 8

M
Malcolm X, 15, 16
Martin, Joe, 5–6, 8, 9

N
Nation of Islam, 15–16, 28

P
Patterson, Floyd, 17

Q
Quarry, Jerry, 21

S
Spinks, Leon, 24

V
Vietnam, 17